PASSIVE INCOME

PASSIVE INCOME

The Exact Strategies For Setting Up 5 Online Businesses That Generate Passive Income

Joshua Ong

© 2018

PASSIVE INCOME

THE EXACT STRATEGIES FOR SETTING UP 5 ONLINE BUSINESSES THAT GENERATE PASSIVE INCOME

© 2018 **JOSHUA ONG**

1st Edition

ALL RIGHTS RESERVED. No part of this book may be reproduced or transmitted in any form whatsoever, electronic, or mechanical, including photocopying, recording, or by any informational storage or retrieval system without expressed written, dated, signed permission from the author.

Author: Joshua Ong

Disclaimer Notice:

Please note the information contained within this document is for educational purposes only. Every attempt has been made to provide accurate, up to date and reliable information. No warranties of any kind are expressed or implied. Readers acknowledge that the author is not engaging in the rendering of legal, financial, medical or professional advice. The content of this book has been derived from various sources. Please consult a licensed professional before attempting any techniques outlined in this book.

By reading this document, the reader agrees that under no circumstances is the author responsible for any losses, direct or indirect, which are incurred as a result of because of he use of information contained within this document, including, but not limited to, errors, omissions, or inaccuracies.

Under no circumstances will any legal responsibility or blame be held against the publisher for any reparation, damages, or monetary loss due to the information herein, either directly or indirectly.

DEDICATION

I dedicate this book to all those who wants something more out of life and refuses to live a mediocre lifestyle and remain status quo; who wants to be the best version of themselves and unleash their full potential; who have dreams and visions to make this world a better place by serving and adding value to others.

I appreciate you and am thankful to you for picking up this book. I believe this book has the power to improve your financial status and finally enabling you to live the lifestyle that you desire. Wishing you all the success in your future endeavors and continue to add value and become an inspiration to the people around you.

To Your Success,
Joshua Ong

CONTENTS

INTRODUCTION	XI
CHAPTER 1: DEVELOPING AN ONLINE COURSE	1
Step 1: Pick the Topic	3
Step 2: Check the Market	3
Step 3: State Learning Outcomes	4
Step 4: Gather the Course Content	5
Step 5: Structure Your Course	6
Step 6: Start Producing Your Course	6
Step 7: Set It All Up	7
Create or Purchase a Logo	8
Udemy vs. Teachable	8
CHAPTER 2: SELL DESIGNER ITEMS ONLINE	15
Step 1: Think about the Products	17
Step 2: Set Your Prices	17
Step 3: Decide Between Creating & Buying	18
Step 4: Set it Up to Sell	18
Step 5: Decide on a Target Audience	19
Step 6: Look at Copyright Responsibility	20
About Product Description	20
Zazzle vs. CafePress	21
Merch by Amazon	22

CHAPTER 3: CREATING A MOBILE APPLICATION — 25

- STEP 1: APP STORE MARKET RESEARCH — 27
- STEP 2: PLAN YOUR IDEA — 27
- STEP 3: DESIGN THE EXPERIENCE — 28
- STEP 4: FIND A DEVELOPER — 28
- STEP 5: START THE PROCESS — 30
- STEP 6: THE TESTING PHASE — 31
- STEP 7: SUBMIT IT TO THE MARKET — 31
- STEP 8: START MARKETING — 32
- HOW MUCH IT COSTS — 32
- QUESTIONS TO ASK YOUR DEVELOPER — 32

CHAPTER 4: WRITING & PUBLISHING AN EBOOK — 39

- STEP 1: START BRAINSTORMING — 40
- STEP 2: CHECK THE MARKET — 41
- STEP 3: START OUTLINING — 42
- STEP 4: START WRITING — 43
- STEP 5: EDITING & FORMATTING — 44
- STEP 6: COVER DESIGN & PUBLISHING — 45
- STEP 7: MARKETING YOUR BOOK — 46
- IF YOU OUTSOURCE YOUR WRITING — 47

CHAPTER 5: AFFILIATE MARKETING — 51

- STEP 1: PICK A NICHE — 52
- STEP 2: START YOUR RESEARCH! — 53
- STEP 3: BUILD YOUR WEBSITE — 54
- STEP 4: PRODUCE CONTENT — 55
- STEP 5: CREATE AN AUDIENCE — 55
- STEP 6: START PROMOTING YOUR LINKS! — 57

HELP WITH AFFILIATE MARKETING — 61

BONUS CHAPTERS — 67

- 4 CORE FUNDAMENTALS OF SUCCESSFUL ONLINE BUSINESS — 67
- TRAFFIC GENERATION — 75

AFTERWORD	79
RESOURCES	85
ACKNOWLEDGMENTS	89
ABOUT THE AUTHOR	90

"Your time is limited, so don't waste it living someone else's life.

Don't be trapped by dogma – which is living with the results of other people's thinking.

Don't let the noise of other's opinions drown out your own inner voice.

And most important, have the courage to follow your heart and intuition."

- Steve Jobs

INTRODUCTION

Why Passive Income and Achieving Financial Freedom

Dear friend,

Why did you decide to pick up this book? Why do you want to start an online business and earn passive income? Since you are reading this book, I believe you have the desire to improve your financial status and earn passive income. This book that you are reading is not just another book you have read about making money online; it is a book about how to achieve financial freedom, your dreams, and goals as well as your aspirations in life. The strategies discussed in this book is just a tool to help you get from where you are currently, to live the life you have always dreamt of living.

I have put this together to help you build your online business and earn passive income in your spare time. Imagine being able to sell anything, anywhere, anytime and even while you are a sleep. Never thought that was possible? Leveraging on the power of the internet will enable you to do that.

In fact, using your spare time to build an online business could potentially earn you a full-time income as well. If you actively read one strategy a day, and take action, you are on your way to building your profitable online business and earning passive income.

No one likes working a nine to five job or living from paycheck to paycheck. Figuring out how to break the cycle is difficult. In this book, you'll learn the exact strategies needed to build up five different online businesses.

Before you get started, you need to understand what passive income is and why every single person needs it.

What is passive income? When you start earning passive income, your time invested is outweighed by what you make. Passive income does not mean that you make income without putting in any work. Often, a passive income stream will require you to put money and time up front to invest in your future earnings. Eventually, your goal is to automate and systemize the entire process, from marketing, payment, fulfillment of orders to following up on your customers.

Why the need for passive income? Simply because you and I only have twenty-four hours per day. And if you are having a job and getting paid based on the hours you work, there will come a time where your income is capped. Your income is capped not because of your performance but because your time is limited, if you are trading time for money. So, the number one rule of earning more money and achieving financial freedom is not having any limits on your income. To bluntly put it, never trade time for money. Because your time is a limited resource and so your income will be limited as well.

Now reading the introduction till this point, you must be wondering how financial freedom is defined as. How I personally define financial freedom is, your passive income is more than your expenses. The two keywords are "passive income" and "expenses". To attain financial freedom faster, simply increase your passive income stream and reduce your expenses. Once you have achieved financial freedom, you technically wouldn't need to work for the rest of your life and you can finally do the things you didn't have the time to do and live the lifestyle of your dreams.

The strategies discussed in this book are tools for you to develop your own stream of passive income and finally enabling you to attain financial freedom. Imagine being able to have freedom in the choices you make without monetary or time constraints. It gives you more choices in life. You are who you are, what you are and where you are because of the past choices you have made on life. Being able to make more choices which you aren't able to in the past due to monetary or time constraints will definitely enable you to go further in life. It will enable you to live your life by design, and not by default.

This is my way of giving back and adding value to you. The strategies I have shared in this book have the potential to set you up for a better life, if you are serious in improving the financial status you are in now and if you take action now!

Do note that this book is not a "Get Rich Quick Scheme", all businesses take effort and time to build. It is actually about building up businesses that will set you up for an entire lifetime.

Now let's get started with the exact strategies to build five online businesses that generate passive income!

> FINANCIAL FREEDOM = PASSIVE INCOME > EXPENSES

What You Need to Do

List down the goals you would like to achieve by the end of this book:

"If you don't find a way to make money while you sleep, you will work until you die."

- Warren Buffett

1

DEVELOPING AN ONLINE COURSE

*"You don't have to be great to get started,
But you have to get started to be great."*

- Les Brown

DEVELOPING AN ONLINE COURSE

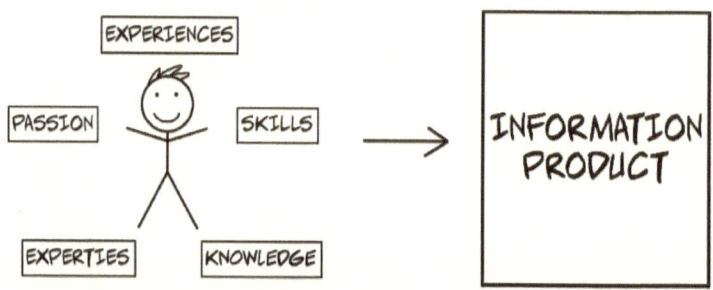

Y ou have something special within you, which you maybe have not used it to its full potential. Ever wonder what it is? It is your skills, knowledge, experiences which you have developed over the years in your career or business. It also could be something which you are very passionate about and spent countless hours geeking and researching about.

These skills, knowledge, experiences and expertise you possess of a certain area is the information needed by someone who is just starting out. In the era of information and technology, it has changed the way how we learn new things. One could just Google search something or YouTube it as well. With the knowledge and expertise you possess you could create an information product and sell it online. There are two ways that you could go about marketing your online course. You can promote your course independently or you can make an online course on an existing platform. In this chapter, we'll cover the two main platforms that you can use to create and market your online course. This will enable you to create a viable stream of passive income leveraging on your expertise.

Step 1: Pick the Topic

You should pick a topic that you love because if you're passionate about a topic, you'll be engaging with the topic. It'll make it easier for you to expand as you already have the skillset and knowledge. Many people can talk about a passionate topic on a single podcast or video, but it takes a level of passion to continue to expand on it enough to develop a course.

It's worth noting that you shouldn't feel compelled to make a college level course, however you need it to be professional. To pick a topic, try to think about what talents, life experiences, and skills you have or have been through. Are you good at writing non-fiction stories? Are you great at interior designing? Do you cook very well? All of these can be topics for an online course. You just need to love the topic, be good at the topic and have useful knowledge, skills, and experiences with it to get started.

Step 2: Check the Market

It'd be great if you could make money on just anything you're passionate about, but nothing is perfect. You still must check to see if there is a high market demand for the topic you have selected. Many people make the mistake of thinking that if there are other courses already on the topic that are gaining a lot of attention, they will not succeed with their own course.

This isn't the case. You need high demand in the market for your course to work. Firstly, check to see if people are talking about it. Next check to see if they are asking questions about it. If they are, then check to see if there is a gap in what the competition is offering? If it exists, you could fill that gap by including it into your course as well. Leverage on this as a unique selling point.

Pro Tip: You could do a search on Google Trends to see which keyword is in demand on the specific topic.

Step 3: State Learning Outcomes

If you want your course to be acceptable, then you need to understand the importance of learning outcomes. If you don't use them, then you risk the reputation and bottom line of your course. No one will hand over money to someone if they don't understand how the product will help them. You must make it clear what you're offering everyone. You may know in your mind what you're offering, but it must be clearly spelled out to other people.

A learning outcome must be explained with measurable verbs what the person will be able to do, feel and know by the end of the course. You need to let them know what knowledge, skills and attitudes they'll learn and be able to demonstrate. For example, if they're going to be confident or lead a healthier lifestyle after the course, you need to make that clear. When you advertise with learning outcomes, you're also attracting the right type of students to enroll in your course. This will help lead to a higher completion and satisfaction rate. In turn, this results in lower refund requests.

Step 4: Gather the Course Content

This is the step where many people start procrastinating and stop getting anything done. The sheer amount of information bouncing around in your head or even just the massive information overload out there can overwhelm you from taking action. You must make sure this does not happen. Start by outlining not only what you should include in your course but you should also decide on what you'll need to leave out. Not everything can be covered in one single course.

Keep your learning outcomes in mind when you're compiling information. Throw out the information that isn't directly related to the learning objectives you've chosen. It's alright to have more than one learning outcome, and you should technically have one for each part of the class. Then just align your content to match it - include content that answers the burning questions your target audience has or fill in any gaps. People are willing to pay for information that you can help simplify, as well as the visuals, unique reflections and new perspective that you offer. Your responsibility is to help the student shorten the steep learning curve.

Step 5: Structure Your Course

Look at your content and start grouping themes, tips and ideas together to fit into modules. This will help you to get the content lined out, and it'll help you to create the following sequence. This is another way to find out if you have any unnecessary information that you need to throw out. It'll also help to show you where you need to expand on.

After you have started structuring your course, you need to determine an effective delivery method for each lesson. There are different principles of adult learning and learning preferences that you need to keep in mind. Engaging content will keep your customers satisfied and better your chances that they'll continue and succeed with the course. Think about what type of visuals you want. Are you going to provide community learning areas so that your students can help each other along? Are you going to have videos, different types of audio content, reading content or activities? You can even create a Facebook Group for your students. These are some of the ways to keep your audience engaged. .

Step 6: Start Producing Your Course

Up until this point, everything has been about planning a course. Now you need to start filming, recording and editing your content. You should have a structured plan on how you're going to deliver the information, what you're going to say, and exactly in what order you plan to say everything. You'll need to buy a good webcam or video camera, have good editing software and have a good microphone for voice recording. Of course, you can always outsource the editing if you have the resources. With so many easy to use webcams out there, your filming can be a DIY (do it yourself). An option can be to outsource the filming.

Pro Tip: If you are shy on camera, you could record your screen and your voice using an application called Movavi or Camtasia.

Step 7: Set It All Up

Think about what platform you want to use. If you had the resources you could even develop your own platform. However, it is easier to try out one of the available platforms out there. These platforms are designed to make the process easier, and they can help you to market your new course as well. One of the easiest platforms to use is Udemy. If you choose Udemy, you'll need a course image, title, subtitle, compelling summary, and you'd need to set the price.

Finally, it's time to publish the course and market it. Marketing will make a large difference in how well it goes. You can hire people to do it for you. Another method is to devise promotional strategies, such as allowing some people access to the course for free in exchange for reviewing it and/or promoting it. You can even join Udemy's Studio U which will connect you with other professors. This will help you grow as an Udemy community, as well as provide you with valuable information that will help both you and your students. It's best to have an eighteen-month marketing plan if you want it to work properly. Think about offering early bird discounts, running advertisements, building a target market list, or even running an affiliate program. It's useful to directly use social media to market, but for the best passive income stream, you might want to eventually outsource your marketing.

Create or Purchase a Logo

Not everyone is confident of designing their own logo, but there's no reason to worry! There are many affordable options out there such as Fiverr where purchasing a logo starts at just $5. There is also 10alogo where you can get a logo or a flat rate of $10. If you want to create a logo quickly and easily by yourself, then try out LogoJoy.

Udemy vs. Teachable

Teachable is another platform that you can use to create an online course and sell it. Let's discuss the pros and cons of both.

The Marketplace: The biggest difference is that Udemy has a marketplace but Teachable does not. For this reason alone, many people choose Udemy. This drives people to their course naturally. With Teachable you'll need to learn a lot more about marketing or pay to get more help.

Pricing: Your pricing strategy is easier with Teachable. You can price your course at whatever amount you want. With Udemy there is a minimum and maximum price.

Competition: Since Teachable does not have a marketplace, you might not be directly competing with other courses on the same platform. With Udemy, you have to compete with other online courses that are advertised right next to yours.

Fees: Udemy charges you depending on how people find your course. If they found it on Udemy, then you're going to get half of what you're asking for. If you send them to Udemy to purchase your course, such as with a coupon code, then you'll get 97% of the profit. If someone recommends your course such as through an affiliate link, then Udemy will only give you 25%. However, with Teachable you pay to create your course. When you sign up, you'll get paid based on the option you chose.

Control: You have more control of your course with Teachable. You can remove your course from Teachable at any time and put it elsewhere. With Udemy, you are not allowed to host your course anywhere else. However, you get to retain the rights to your course.

Mailing List: Udemy will also prohibit you from creating your own mailing list. This is a common back-end marketing tactic to increase your passive income. Teachable does not prohibit you from doing so.

Reviews: Reviews will matter differently depending on which option you go with. With Udemy, everything is dependent on reviews. This is where promotional tools come in handy during the early publishing stages of your course. Teachable does not put as much pressure on you to get reviews, but reviews will make it easier for you to sell your course.

Affiliates: Udemy will give 50% the person that's recommending your course, but Teachable will allow you to choose the way you like to split the earnings.

What You Need to Do

1) Brainstorming your niche market:
    a) What are you truly passionate about? (hobbies, interest, etc.)

    b) What are the skills you have learnt? (education, career, etc.)

    c) What topic do you enjoy learning about?

d) What are the problems faced by the people who are asking for your advice?

P.s Based on the questions you have answered above, decide on **one** area you are most passionate about to develop a course.

2) Do a market research and indicate the competitors in your niche and their gaps:

P.s Identify the gaps of your competitors and include it in your course.

3) State the learning outcomes of your course:

4) Outline the contents of your course

5) Determine an effective method of delivery and how to make it engaging (i.e Animation, Whiteboard, Handouts):

6) Start producing your course:
   - ☐ Script
   - ☐ Recording
   - ☐ Editing

7) Setting it up:
   - ☐ Name of your course
   - ☐ Logo
   - ☐ Platform to market (i.e Udemy, Teachable, Others)
   - ☐ Pricing
   - ☐ Marketing

"You will never leave where you are until you decide where you'd rather be."

- Dexter Yager

2

SELL DESIGNER ITEMS ONLINE

"Design creates culture.

Culture shapes values.

Values determine the future."

- Robert L. Peters

DESIGNING ON MERCHANDISE

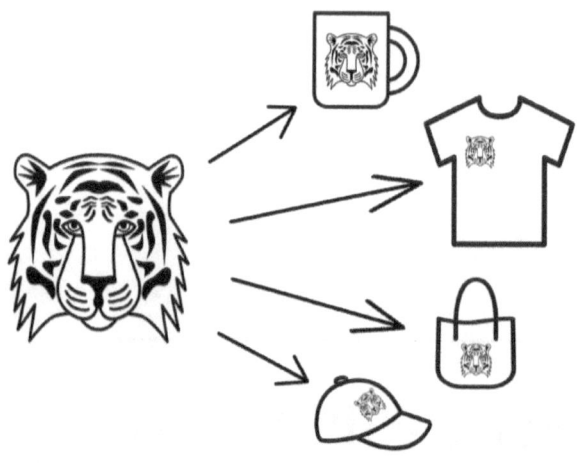

Have you ever purchased something before just because it had a really nice design and art work? There are many ways that you can use your designing and creative abilities to make passive income online. There are countless websites out there that can give you a platform to sell and create your items. CafePress and Zazzle are the top popular platforms, but some people will use Merch by Amazon as well. In this chapter, we will use CafePress as an example of how to get started.

Step 1: Think about the Products

The first thing you need to do after creating an account is that you'll need to create your own CafePress store. You then need to design logos to go on each product. You'll earn royalties on everything that you sell. What makes CafePress such an appealing option is that there are no upfront costs that you must pay to create your own store. With any of these options, you also don't have to concern yourself with keeping any inventory. Everything is made as per purchase, and the company just takes a percentage of the amount that it's sold for. Currently, CafePress has over 250 products that you can choose from to start selling.

Step 2: Set Your Prices

There is a base price that CafePress has for all their items. You'll then markup that price as necessary. When you sell the item, you're receiving the markup price. Just consider the base price before you figure out how much you want from each item. If they're selling a shirt for $15, then a markup of $10 can be too high. Instead, you may want to consider just a $5 markup on the shirt to keep it within a reasonable budget for your customers. It's all about finding the sweet spot in pricing.

There are other ways you can make money with this platform as well. If you sell over $100 in products, including the minimum of the base price, you can get a bonus that ranges from 10% to 30%. You'll also get a bonus of 10% if you allow your products to be sold in CafePress marketplace. Setting up a shop will cost either a 10% deduction from your royalties each month, which won't exceed $10, or you can prepay for a little under $7 a month. If you decide to pay for a total year, it's only $5 each month. .

Step 3: Decide Between Creating & Buying

You may have already dismissed this idea if you're not an artist or if you feel you can't put the time into designing. You can either outsource the creation of your logos, which will be pricey for commercial use, or you can create them yourself. You don't even have to be a designer to create these photos either. You can just use graphics programs like GIMP or Photoshop with a minimal amount of creativity.

GIMP is a free software. However, you're more limited with what you can do with GIMP compared to Photoshop, and they aren't self-explanatory programs. You'll need some time to understand how they work and get the hang of it. PicMonkey is also a great alternative since it's easier to use than either Photoshop or GIMP since it's created with beginners in mind. Coming up with funny sayings and slogans can work in your favor too.

Step 4: Set it Up to Sell

You still haven't gotten to the passive part of this passive income stream. You still need to market your items. Link your shop with websites or blogs that have some traffic. You may also fill out all of your titles, subtitle, and descriptions with SEO content so that it will be more likely search engines will pick up on your product. You can also run ads, but all of that can be outsourced. Eventually, you'll be making more than just what's equal to the time you put into the original design. It should slow down to only a few hours a week!

Step 5: Decide on a Target Audience

If you're still having trouble selling your t-shirts or other products online, then you're going to want to ask yourself if you're targeting the right audience. You'll need to ask yourself a few questions to determine who you want your audience to be.

- Do you want more males or females to buy your products?

- What age group do you want to buy your products?

- Do you want it to appeal to the mainstream or a subgroup of people?

- Do you want to cater towards a mass appeal or to a niche such as gothic humor?

- Are you targeting a low, middle or high-income person?

All these questions will pull your shop together and serve a specific target market. When you answer these questions, you'll know what price to sell the product at, what images will appeal to the people you're trying to sell to, what types of colors to use, and even what particular products may sell the best. It'll also help you decide if you want to specialize or not. There are many shops that specialize in niches such as weddings, anniversaries, outdoors, or even tribal designs.

Step 6: Look at Copyright Responsibility

It's your responsibility to ensure copyright on any of these platforms. You can use free stock images or even slogans and phrases that aren't copyrighted. It's important to know where you're getting your images from, especially if you're outsourcing the design work. There are many free stock photos available online, such as Stocksnap.io, Upsplash, Pexels, and Gratisography to start with. Words and phrases aren't copyrighted, but they may be trademarked, which is just as bad. If you want to check a trademark on a word or phrase, then you'll want to check the public trademark registry.

About Product Description

Your product description should have Search Engine Optimization(SEO) so that your product can be found. It'll help to bring people to your storefront or to your page on your platform. If you're still having trouble with SEO after researching it, you might want to check out a few free SEO tools. Try SERanking, Wordstream Free Keyword Tool, or even Microsoft's free SEO toolkit.

Zazzle vs. CafePress

We've used CafePress as an example, but now it's time to look at the other popular platforms. Just like with CafePress, you'll need to start by making an account and take care of setting up a store. Here are some tips on the differences between Zazzle and CafePress that may be able to help you choose the program that fits you.

Pricing: CafePress doesn't let you set up your own royalties, but Zazzle does. You can set anything between ten percent to thirty-five percent. However, it has a minimum payment threshold for PayPal which is $50. If you want to get paid out before that, then you need to pay a $2.50 fee. For a cheque to be issued, the minimum is $100 or a $5 charge before you meet the threshold. CafePress offers a flat ten percent royalty on your product. The minimum payment threshold is $25 as well for either PayPal or cheque. Just remember that CafePress does allow you to earn performance bonuses!

Affiliate Programs: The minimum commission for a referral is fifteen percent with Zazzle, but it can go up to thirty percent. CafePress only does an affiliate program from their marketplace, so you need to make sure that you have the right link.

Merch by Amazon

Now that you know the pros and cons of Zazzle and CafePress, you'll want to compare it to Merch by Amazon. Here are a few things that this platform has to offer.

Pros:

T-shirt Templates: Just in case you might be thinking about selling your own T-Shirts online and if you're having an issue with designing your t-shirt, you can download a t-shirt template with Illustrator, GIMP, or Photoshop

Brand: You can sell the Amazon brand, which is what many people trusts.

Prime Membership: Amazon Prime members will receive shipping perks on your items. This will drive more business to you.

Cons:

Invitation Only: You have to request an invitation from Merch by Amazon in order to join which is subject to their approval.

T-shirts Only: You are only able to sell t-shirts with this service.

No Brand Identity: Customers won't know who designed the shirt. They just will know that it's sold by Amazon.

What You Need to Do

1) List down the various type of merchandise you would like to sell:

2) Setting it up:
- ☐ Getting your logo / artwork done
- ☐ Identify the price of your product: $ _____
- ☐ Ensure there is no copyrights issue

3) Write the description of your product:

4) List your target market (i.e Youths, Entrepreneurs, Gothic, Sporty etc) and the age range:

5) Identify the platform you would be using to promote your items:
- ☐ Merch by Amazon
- ☐ CafePress
- ☐ Zazzle
- ☐ Others: _____

"Good artists copy, great artists steal."

- Pablo Picasso

3

CREATING A MOBILE APPLICATION

"The future of mobile apps is now."

- Unknown

MOBILE APP

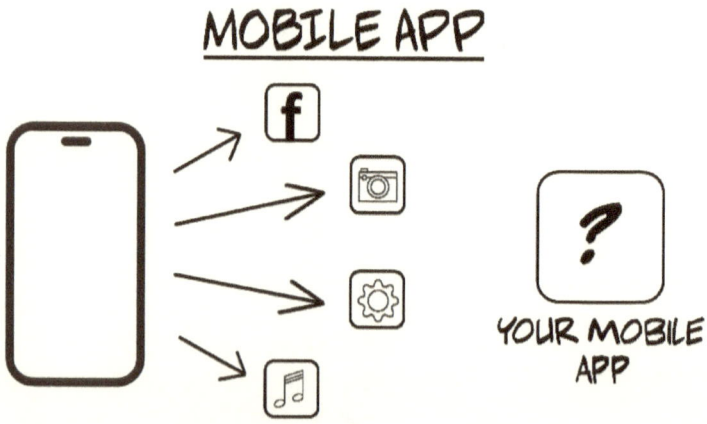

You would probably have countless mobile apps that you use throughout the day and you know that all of these apps make money somehow. At some point of time I am very sure you would have downloaded a free-to-play game and somehow started watching a video advertisement just to gain some incentive in the game. When you get hooked in playing and wanting to win, you would end up spending real money in purchasing more coins or gems in the game. I call this free-to-play and pay-to-win. I know this because, I have spent money on a game as well.

Well, have you ever had a great idea for an app but never took it anywhere? You should make that app and finally sell it! All you have to decide is if you're going to create it yourself or hire a programmer to create it. Then all you need to do is create the app, list it and collect income per paid download, advertising fees or even sell your app in the app store and collect the residual income.

Step 1: App Store Market Research

As with any successful business, you will need to research the market for your app. You must understand the marketplace if you want your app to sell. You can always check out the top paid, top free, and top grossing apps in real time at the Apple store or you may want to check the apps out on Android. This depends on where you want to sell your app. Just review the charts frequently and write down the potential trends that you spot. If you do this repeatedly, then you'll learn what a successful app idea and design looks like. You are also likely to think about the marketing aspect of your app. You might want to write down the various pricing models. This research costs you nothing, and it's simple to do.

Step 2: Plan Your Idea

Ask yourself if the app you're creating is similar to the apps that are in the top apps chart? If you find apps that are similar, then you have a potential seller on your hands. If you don't see it there, then there likely isn't a big market for the app you want to create. You need to emulate existing apps if you want to be successful. Too often people fall in love with their own idea even if there isn't a market for it. There is nothing wrong in wanting to create something different, but I personally never suggest to try and "Reinvent the Wheel". Plan out all the features you want to be included in your app. To do this, you may want to download a few of the apps that you want to model after or that has a really great user experience.

Step 3: Design the Experience

This stage is when you have to create a draft of your app. Don't worry, we aren't going to design it yet! You can even just draw it on a sheet of paper, but you need to make it tangible in some way. Use those apps you want to model, and then look to see what functionalities you want from it.

Take components of apps you feel work well and model them like you did the idea. You can give these ideas to your programmer, but you need to make what you're expecting as clear as possible. The clearer you are with your programmer, the easier it will be for them to create an app that meets your expectations. You can even take screenshots of other apps to submit to your developer.

Step 4: Find a Developer

Once your idea is all planned out, it's time to find a developer for the platform you're looking to create the app on. Of course, don't let the word developer intimidate you. You just need a programmer who knows what they're doing. You should always start by finding someone who can develop on Apple iOS first, as it has a higher chance of succeeding than an Android statistically. Depending on what type of app you want, you'll need to make sure that the developer knows how to do it.

Different codes will produce something different. There is Python, PHP, Ruby, Java, Go, C#, and Lua. Of course, if you explain what you want your app to do clearly, the programmer will know if they know the right coding language to produce what you desire. Here are a few places you might want to check out to find a suitable developer for what you want.

Here are the two best freelancer websites to look at. However, if you're willing to pay more you can also consider getting a company to pay for their services. Though, when working with a freelancer, decide in advance if you're looking for someone that you pay by the hour or if you're looking for someone that will work for a flat rate.

Upwork: Formerly known as Elance, Upwork is a great place to find various freelancers, so it should be easy to find a developer for your app. You'll just post a job proposal, marking your budget, and then you wait for people to bid on your job post. You will then review their applications and decide on the person you feel is best qualified.

Freelancer: This works the same as Upwork, so remember that it's important to be as specific as possible when describing your job so that you can find the best fit.

Pro Tip: If you have no coding background but want to develop an app yourself you can check out Appery or AppMachine.

Step 5: Start the Process

You don't always want to dump the workload on your developer, especially if you have any reservations about hiring them. Start with a few smaller tasks so that you can accurately assess how good their coding skills are as well as the speed they can work at comfortably. It also helps you to get a look at their overall work dynamic, so you know exactly what you're getting in for since you have a big project ahead of you.

If you don't find their skills to be good enough, then you want to get out quickly. If you do that, then you'll just pay them for the work they already did before it starts to accumulate. During the coding process, you should ask them to create and deliver an icon for your app. If you have several ideas, pass it to them so they know what direction you want to go in. You can also ask for a demonstration app.

Often referred to as a "Hello, World" app because it has an opening page that says "Hello, World!", and it takes about ten minutes to create. This will determine how the developer delivers the app for you to test. You also can get an idea of what the icon will look on your phone. The next step is the actual delivery of your app. You'll need an "ad hoc" version so that you can run your app on your phone without needing to download it from an App Store.

Step 6: The Testing Phase

Your developer shouldn't be the only one that tests out your app. You should too! You can then see if there are any questions that need to be addressed, errors or even design flaws that you want to be worked out before you have them sent in. Also, you should never assume that something works just because you tested it once before. Every time you get an updated version of your app, you need to make sure that the update doesn't cause issues with features that previously worked. You don't have to be the only tester either. Your app will immediately make sense to you, but you need an outside perspective.

Pro Tip: You could get your friends to "Beta Test" your app as well so you could get some feedback.

Step 7: Submit it to the Market

You'll need to outline in your original agreement whose responsibility it is to submit your app to the marketplace. It's best to have your programmer take it over or just show you how to submit it so that you can do it yourself from now on. Usually, a company will require you to wait seven to ten days before you get an answer.

Step 8: Start Marketing

It can be stressful to try to breakthrough and have a successful app. It all boils down to your marketing. This task belongs to you and not your developer. After you have an app that has a seamless flow from the icon to the way to download and use it, it's important to start getting your payout there. Find different ways to run ads to get people to download and review it.

How Much It Costs

How much it costs will depend on how much you want in your app. Though with UPwork the usual price is under $800 for the project, so there are many times that you can get a normal app made for under $1,000. It just depends on what you want and who you get to make your app. There are some developers that will charge a few thousand or more to actually create an app with all of the effects that some apps need. It all depends on you but think about the cost in comparison to how much money you realistically plan to make off of it.

Questions to Ask Your Developer

Before we move on to the next section, you may still feel nervous about finding a developer for your app. Here are some questions that you can ask your developer before hiring them. You can even put these in the job description so that they answer you right away!

a) What are some examples you can provide me?

A qualified candidate should have a list of apps they are responsible for creating or had a major role in developing. They should have links to each of the apps that they have developed before that you can check out. Examples are important for a freelancer. Don't let someone's affordability fool you. If they don't have the examples to back it up they may not be legitimate. You can't gauge their skill level without it.

b) Do you have a list of current and past clients?

The examples are great, but there is no way to tell if their examples are legitimate if you can't speak to their current and past clients. Checking references will also let you know how responsive, result oriented and reliable the person is. You can ask if they stayed within budget, delivered within the deadline, or even if they work well under pressure. Just take it with a pinch of salt because they often will only offer you references that make them look better.

c) What type of phone do you have?

You should know if they have an iPhone or an Android. You'll want someone who is using the apps for the platform they're saying they can build for. If they use them on a regular basis, then they have a firsthand account of how apps usually work and the problems that the platform has.

d) How do you prefer to communicate when working together?

It's important to know how you're going to communicate with the person you're working with. If you prefer frequent updates, it's best to get someone who works well with that type of schedule. If you're someone who has everything planned out at the beginning and only wants them to contact you with questions, then you don't need to be as worried about communication. You just need to know how to get hold of them effectively and during what days and hours.

e) Are you good at creating any type of special features?

It can be hard for an app to find success without having some sort of special feature that can grab the consumer's attention. Can they add 3-D gaming for example? Perhaps social media sharing, GPS check-ins or product coupons to your app?

f) How will it be tested?

You should know how your app is going to be tested too. You should never be given an app that has glitches. They should be able to weed out bugs and you should know how long it'll take them to do so.

g) Who owns it when it's done?

Typically, you should own your mobile app when it's done. They should not be able to make any further income from it, and you'll need to have a copyright assignment for that. Therefore, it should be clear they're working a work made for hire basis.

h) Who takes care of the submission process?
Ask your developer if they're going to handle submitting the app to the app stores. If it's been beta-tested, then there's no reason they shouldn't want to. It should just be listed as part of the job since app submission can be a multi-step process that takes some time. It can be hard to successfully navigate the process if you don't know what you're doing.

What You Need to Do

1) Brainstorm your mobile application idea and list down what would be the function of your application:

2) Market research the app store and list down other applications similar to your mobile application idea:

3) Draft out the design and the experience (draw out the page layouts):

4) Determine which developer you would be using:

<u>Outsourcing</u>

- ☐ Upwork
- ☐ Fiverr
- ☐ Freelance
- ☐ Others: _____
- ☐

<u>Develop it yourself</u>

- ☐ Appery
- ☐ AppMachine
- ☐ Others: _____

5) Determine your monetization model:

- ☐ Banner Ads
- ☐ Full-page Ads
- ☐ Cost per install
- ☐ In-app purchase

6) Setting it up:

- ☐ Testing the app out and finalizing it
- ☐ Something the app to the market
- ☐ Marketing your app

"All our dreams can come true if we have the courage to pursue them."

- Walt Disney

4

WRITING & PUBLISHING AN EBOOK

"Whatever the mind of man can conceive and believe, it can achieve."

- **Napoleon Hill**

WRITING A BOOK

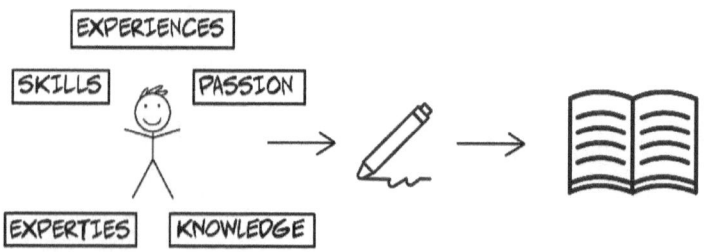

This is one of the tried and true methods of passive income. There are many successfully self-published books out there that are rolling in the cash, and there are even courses to help you learn everything you need to know. This chapter will get you started in the right direction. In this chapter, we're mainly going to focus on you writing your own eBook, but you can hire out, which will be discussed at the end.

Step 1: Start Brainstorming

The first thing you'll need to do is to start brainstorming on what you want your book to be about. Many people will choose something they're passionate about so that they can write on it. After all, if you write your own eBook then you save money too, which means that this passive income stream will have a smaller startup cost. Think about what you like to do, and then come up with a list of ideas on what you can write about. Are you passionate about fitness? Do you love to cook? Do you enjoy dancing? Do you have a hobby that you're knowledgeable about such as hunting or fishing? These are all viable options to write on. Let's take gardening for example.

Step 2: Check the Market

You need to check the market to see if you'll be able to sell the book you want to write on. Sticking to gardening as an example, are their gardening books in the top 100 downloaded books from popular platforms such as Kindle? Are they paid for or free books that are in a program like Kindle Unlimited? If the answer is yes, then you can continue with a gardening book.

However, what types of gardening books are popular right now? Is it a beginner's gardening book or is it on something specific such as sustainable gardening? Gardening will be a niche, and then you'll just need to choose a sub-niche. To pick a second category, which is your sub-niche, you need to recognize that you're looking at keywords. Sustainable gardening would be a keyword. Here is a list of other possible keywords you might see:

- ☐ Sustainable Gardening
- ☐ Homesteading Garden
- ☐ Gardening for Beginner's
- ☐ Gardening for the Busy Mom
- ☐ Container Gardening
- ☐ Hydroponics Gardening

You may not know about most of these but pick one you do feel you know enough about. Do you grow most of your plants in pots instead of the ground? Then try writing on container gardening or sustainable gardening if you have rows of vegetables and fruits that grow back every year. Now that you've selected another category, you can move on to step three.

Step 3: Start Outlining

Now that you know what you want to write about, which for this example is container gardening, you need to start outlining your book. Here's an example of what your outline could look like. Remember that this is just your template for writing, so just jot everything down under your chapter titles for now.

Introduction: You'll need to introduce your book and why you're writing it.
Why Container Gardening: Explain why people should use containers and who it benefits.
Best Containers to Use: Start getting down to the meat of the topic. Not every container is created equal after all. Tell them why you use what you do or don't use.
Best Plants to Grow: There are some plants that grow well in confined spaces and some that grow poorly, so make sure you give your readers the best chance at success.
Some FAQ: This will help you to answer remaining questions that they might have.

Best Soil & Fertilizer: This will help to explain how to get your plants to prosper.

Some Extra Tips: Do you have anything else to add to the topic? This would be a great way to add it and give your readers a little more information!

Conclusion: Reiterate your points and thank them for buying your book.

With the outline above, you've given them a way to get hooked on your book which is your introduction, you've taken them through common questions, and you've gone over the steps it takes to build a container garden. After that, you gave a few more helpful tips to help them be successful, which their success will equal better reviews for you, and you've wrapped the book up in a conclusion.

You can do this with any topic! Remember that it's okay to do a little research to fill in any gaps you may have about the topic. If your research is thorough, you don't always have to talk from firsthand experience. It's just easier to write your first book about something you know a lot about.

Step 4: Start Writing

This part may be self-explanatory, but there are some tips that will make the process easier. First off, you should be aware of your word count even if you're writing yourself. Try to figure out what books sell best. If you're just testing the waters, books from 6,000 to 10,000 words are a great way to go. However, if you want more long-term results, then longer books tend to sell better. Try to write a book that's 15,000 to 25,000 words long. Your words directly relate to your page count, and people want to feel like they're getting their money's worth.

If you're selling a book for $5 for an eBook copy, then you're going to need to have the pages to back it up. If it's under twenty-five pages, you're going to want to sell it for a lot less. Now that you've figured out the word count that you want, then assign a word count to each chapter so that you don't end up rambling. Don't be worried if you go a little over on each chapter, but try not to go under.

Step 5: Editing & Formatting

You'll need to edit your book with Microsoft Word. This becomes easier since it does have a spelling and grammar check. You need to understand that it will only catch misspelled words. For example, you may have meant to write "she ate the" but spelled "she ape the". It will not catch this. That's why it's important to go through your document with a fine-tooth comb or hire someone to do it for you. After that, you need to format it for whatever platform you want to publish on. Also, an eBook is formatted differently than a print book that you'd want to sell through CreateSpace, but both are technically an Amazon process.

Pro Tip: You can check your grammar for free using Grammarly

Step 6: Cover Design & Publishing

Before you can publish there is one more thing you need to do! You'll need to get a cover designed. One of the best places to do this is through Fiverr. You can get a Kindle eBook cover for as little as $5, and often takes only three days! For cover design, keep these tips in mind. .

Title & Subtitle: You should already have this by this point, and it should have good keywords in it so that it's easy for people to find your book.
Thumbnail: Your design should look good in a thumbnail, so if a cover is too busy it'll look messy. People will be browsing your book via thumbnail.
Photo Rights: You should either have rights to the photos that your designer is using or your designer should be using free stock photos.

If you're looking to publish on Kindle, then everything is a little easier because there are various tutorials out there that will teach you what to do. With Kindle, it only takes about five minutes to publish your book. You'll just need to fill out the description, which should be riddled with SEO too so that it can easily be found in the Amazon search engine.

As far as pricing goes, you'll need to set it when you publish your book. With Kindle you'll be able to choose how large of a royalty you get from each sale. Amazon will let you choose a 35% royalty or a 70% royalty, but you have to check out the price requirements for each. If you want to set the price, then you usually need to go with the 35% royalty. If you have no issue with Amazon's suggested price, then you can earn a 70% royalty. However, the 70% royalty requires that you sell your book higher.

Step 7: Marketing Your Book

You'll need to market your book if you want to succeed! You can't just set it up on Kindle or another platform and expect it to sell itself. If you have your SEO done, then you're going to get a few sales, but you won't start making a large passive income stream until you start marketing it. It also helps, if you to have many books that you've published before. There is a trend that shows that if an author has twenty books, then they're more likely to be considered an authority in the niche so long as those books are within the same relative category. You may want to join review groups as well to get reviews for your book in exchange for a promotional copy. You can also take advantage of the promotions that Kindle Direct Publishing lets you use to sell your book too!

Pro Tip: You can publish your book on Amazon in multiple formats such as Kindle, paperback and audio as well. If you self-publish your book on Amazon via CreateSpace, and when someone makes a purchase, Amazon will deal with the order fulfillment.

If You Outsource Your Writing

If you outsource your writing you're going to need a larger startup, but it does mean less work for you which will make this much more passive. You'll want to check out the same freelance websites that were recommended for developing a mobile app. Just find a freelancer that's within your budget. The standard price is $10-$15 per 1,000 words. Keep this in mind when you're budgeting for your book. If you outsource your book, then you're only responsible for the marketing! Just make sure that the book you get is copyright free so that there are no issues later on. You might want to try PlagScan or CopyScape to check for plagiarism before you mark the job as complete.

What You Need to Do

1) State your passion, strengths and interest:

P.s Based on your passion, strengths and interest identify **one** area you would like to write your book on. You could refer to your answers filled in first chapter of this book as well.

2) Do a market research and indicate the best sellers eBooks in your niche:

Book Title	Book Ranking

3) Identify the keywords used in your specific niche:

4) Write down the outline of your book:

5) Setting it up:
 - ☐ Writing your book
 - ☐ Editing and Formatting
 - ☐ Designing your cover
 - ☐ Publishing your book
 - ☐ Marketing your book

"You must be willing to do the things today others don't do, in order to have the things tomorrow others won't have."

- Les Brown

5

AFFILIATE MARKETING

"Don't find customers for your product. Find products for your customers."

- Seth Godin

AFFILIATE MARKETING WITH A BLOG

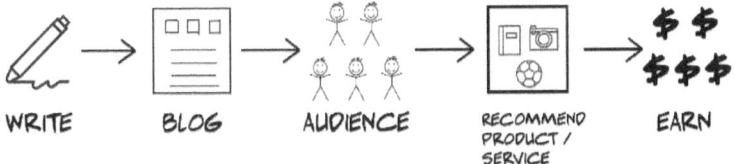

WRITE → BLOG → AUDIENCE → RECOMMEND PRODUCT / SERVICE → EARN

Most people understand how bloggers make money. They build an audience that trusts them, and then they offer services or products that help that audience. Affiliate marketing is a quicker way to offer products and services without having to worry about creating them yourself. It's all about getting a commission on a sale. You introduce your readers to services or products that are from trusted individuals or companies. If you're a blogger, this means finding a product or service you feel comfortable promoting to your readers. In this chapter, we will discuss how to be an affiliate marketer by using a blog.

Step 1: Pick a Niche

Start by picking a niche you feel you can write on, which is best if you don't have enough capital to outsource everything right away. This will be a similar process to choosing something to write on for Kindle, so just go through the steps. The difference is that you'll want to get at least twenty different article topics ready to see if you'll have enough to talk about for quite some time to come. Remember that building a good blog means that you need to be able to answer something for your audience and learn to keep them engaged.

Step 2: Start Your Research!

Now instead of researching your niche, you need to research what affiliate programs you'd like to recommend to your audience. You shouldn't be afraid to invest time in choosing the right program, service or product to promote to your followers. Promoting the right thing will pay off later in the long term. Keep in mind that you would only want to be promoting something which is trustable and legitimate. The best way to identify whether the product is legitimate is by personally purchasing it and testing it out. After doing so, you could then write a review about it as well. You may want to check out which marketplace or platform you would want to work with as well. ClickBank is a popular platform for merchants to list their products on and for affiliates to promote. You also need to look at how much commission you'll make per sale. Affiliate for programs that are profitable, meaning the merchant offer over 50% commission and also gives you the back-end sales.

If you're going to choose a cost per action program (CPA), then you should ensure that the that commissions are at least over a dollar. Otherwise, you'll just be making pennies. You also need to make sure they aren't going to restrict how you promote them. If you're going to be selling a physical product, the commission should be over $40 to make it worth your time. Also, ask yourself if you want to be associated with what you're selling. You also need to make sure that you fully understand the support that the merchant will provide you. What kind of customer support can you expect once you've become an affiliate marketer? Try to speak to other sellers to get your thoughts together, and ask if you can contact people via Skype or phone. Do you have to email them and wait a few days for a response?

Step 3: Build Your Website

Now that you've gotten your research together, it's time to start building your website. Building a website isn't as labor-intensive or complicated as people think. Most people will choose to do it all on their own, but you can pay someone to do it for you. Remember that Upwork is a great way to do that if you choose to outsource this part! However, if it's your first time building a website you may want to try WordPress. WordPress CMS is easy to use, and you don't need coding skills. Just buy a domain which will be the address to your website. You should have several options in mind because it's likely that a few of them have already been taken.

GoDaddy is a popular way to buy a domain name, so is NameCheap. The domain is your address, but you need a hosting service as well. You can think of this hosting service as your house. It's where your site will live, and it's your slice of the internet. Hosting is affordable, so go with a reliable and reputable provider. GoDaddy does provide hosting as well, but HostGator and BlueHost are two recommended hosting sites as well. If the domain and hosting are purchased separately, you can link them together quickly. CMS installation is next to where you install WordPress, then you choose your theme, and only then can you start creating your content.

Step 4: Produce Content

Now that your website is up and running, you need to produce content to keep your audience hooked. The more valuable content you provide the more your audience will trust what you're marketing. This is the most time-consuming part of affiliate marketing if you are using a blog. Think about your niche and what you can write about. Remember that your content will need to be churned out on a regular basis to keep your audience involved. Some people even choose to make their website about product reviews, which is considered an easy way to become an authority in your niche and seamlessly promote products that you're affiliated with too. You can either write the content yourself through research and experience or you can use freelance websites such as Upwork to outsource this task.

Step 5: Create an Audience

Some people will come naturally if you've encoded keywords, also known as search engine optimization (SEO) into your content, but this won't be enough. You need to actively create an audience, but with a virtual assistant, this can later be outsourced as well. You'll want to promote your content using social media such as Instagram, Pinterest, Twitter and even Facebook. There are other location-specific networks as well. You will want to create a Facebook page to help promote your content too! You will want to use the following techniques too.

Guest Posting: Try to guest post on high traffic blogs. This will allow you to capitalize on someone else's audience, and therefore you can focus on your own content a little more. Try to contact some high traffic blogs that are in a niche similar to yours. You'll be writing content for a larger site, but you get their audience because of it.

Email Lists: An email list is crucial if you want to be a successful affiliate marketer. Use lead magnets, where you are promoting information products for free, or just by encouraging people to sign up for updates. Then you'll be able to push your content to an audience through your email list. Just make sure that you aren't too sleazy with your sales. Build up trust, and then purchasing from you will come naturally.

SEO Techniques: It increases your chances of being found. You'll either need to learn SEO yourself or you'll need to hire an SEO marketer, which can also be a freelancer to save you money.

Paid Advertising: Paid advertising can pay off if you have the right content, product, a good sales process with high commissions!

Pro Tip: Master one paid advertising platform and focus on it, you could consider advertising on Facebook, Google or Bing.

Step 6: Start Promoting Your Links!

This is where marketing your affiliate links actually comes up. Once you've proven you have value to add to your niche, you can start promoting products to the audience that you created. There are ways to promote your offers, such as product reviews. Write real reviews that are honest about your products, and build up trust. Remember that you are giving them something to rely on when making their decision. You shouldn't just gloss over the negatives because of it. An honest review will be a valued review. You should also mention useful features, add compelling images, and make sure that you don't skimp on the details.

Banner ads are also a way to promote your affiliate offers. These can be provided to you by your affiliate company. You'll just need to insert their banner on your page, but make sure that you pick the right locations. You can link things in text too. For example, if you're talking about a hairdryer, you'd then create a hyperlink to your affiliate product with the word hairdryer. Email promotions we've already covered, but giveaways and discounts are another great idea too. If you run a promotion or good discount, your product becomes attractive to the audience. Just stick to it and find the right program, service or product for you and your audience!

Pro Tip: If you think it is too much of a hassle to create your own website, you could promote your affiliate links by doing a review on YouTube, Facebook and Instagram as well with your affiliate link in the description.

What You Need to Do

1) Decide on the Niche you would like to be in:

Pro Tip: The 3 Best Niches to be in is something related to Health, Wealth Creation or Relationship.

2) Research on Clickbank, JVzoo or other platforms on the available affiliate programs in the niche that you have chosen:

AFFILIATE MARKETING | 59

3) Building up your website:

- ☐ Decide a name for the blog, site or company
- ☐ Purchase domain name on GoDadddy
- ☐ Connect domain to a website builder

4) Brainstorm some content ideas for your website:

5) Create your audience:

- ☐ SEO
- ☐ Guest Posting
- ☐ Paid Advertising
- ☐ Banner Ads
- ☐ Others: _____

6) Finally, actually start promoting your links.

"If you want to be successful, find someone who has achieved the results you want and copy what they do and you'll achieve the same results."

- Tony Robbins

HELP WITH AFFILIATE MARKETING

You still might have no idea what affiliate marketing is or where to start, I hope this chapter will clear things for you. Many people get discouraged with affiliate marketing if they don't get it right the first time, but there are always ways to make it easier! In this chapter, we're going to go over a few resources that you can use to help build up this type of passive income stream.

ClickBank

ClickBank is easy to use, and it's one of the most common affiliate platforms that people start out with. Of course, that doesn't mean you have to start out with them. Though they're easy to make an account with, and you get paid every two weeks! You should never promote a product that you don't think your audience will buy. The ClickBank Marketplace has hundreds of products for you to choose from, but keep in mind that not all products are worth promoting. Being able to determine which product to promote is essential because you would be spending time, effort or money to promote it, so it should be worth your while.

Selecting Quality and Best-Selling Products on ClickBank

Gravity

ClickBank uses a term called "Gravity" to represent how well the product is selling. This is based on the total sales made and also if there are any recent sales. A gravity of 0 to 50 is rather considered Low Gravity. A High Gravity would be above 100, which would indicate that the sales are good, thus there would be a higher competition in the specific niche. Competition meaning there are many other affiliate marketers out there which are promoting the same product, and you would have to go against them. However, competition does not necessarily have a negative connotation to it. It also means that there is a lot of demand for that specific product. On the other hand, a product with Low Gravity could just mean that it is a brand-new product or a hidden gem.

Pro Tip: Select a product with a gravity more than 100. I would recommend to promote a product that already works and has a demand rather than spending time to test something new.

Commission Percentage

Make sure the product you choose to affiliate gives out more than 50% commission.

Up and Down Sells

Choose an affiliate product which has a sales funnel in place. A sales funnel technically means that after a purchase as been made for the front-end product, the vendor would promote an "upgrade" or add-ons at the back end. A product which has a couple of up and down-sells would lead to higher commissions.

Quality Marketing Materials

The vendor should provide high quality marketing materials such as email swipes and banner ads at no cost. You can check the marketing materials under "vendor spotlight" or click the link stating "affiliates".

Converting Vendor Pitch Page

Ensure you have went through the landing page of the offer you will be promoting. The landing page should persuasive enough that people would purchase the product.

Being able to choose the right product to promote is the first step of being a successful affiliate marketer. If you do it right, you can drastically improve your potential of earning a good income. Remember, don't just set up your offer page and forget all about it. Monitor your ClickBank reports and also using Tracking IDs to see which marketing strategy and product are performing the best so you know where to focus your efforts and resources.

JVZoo

With JVZoo there are two ways you can receive your commission which is either by cheque or PayPal. If you choose to get paid through PayPal you'll get your money immediately after the sale has been processed! This can be great, but you need to keep in mind that if someone comes back to request a refund, then JVZoo will take the money back from you too. For this reason, it's usually best to avoid using the money until you feel it's unlikely someone will request a refund or until it passes the refund window period. When you're picking a product from the marketplace, there are a few things to look out for too. You'll want to find the product and then click on it. You need to see if it's a long-term affiliate product or if the product is expired. Keep in mind that they're listed by popularity. Each product will have a different commission rate too.

Amazon

Keep in mind that the minimum payment threshold for Amazon is $100. You'll either be paid through direct deposit, a cheque which does have a fee, or you can choose to get paid in an Amazon gift card! Signing up with Amazon affiliate is just as easy as the previous two methods. However, it's important to note that they do usually take longer to approve you, and they have been known to be pickier about who they let in. This means it's important that you have a high traffic website before you apply. Amazon does not provide you with any learning material to use their affiliate programs successfully, but if you have a basic understanding of affiliate programs you should be fine. Just remember to choose the product that appeals to your niche and your audience.

ClickFunnels

If you are looking for an opt-in or landing page builder, ClickFunnels is what you should be looking for. They have a very seamless drag and drop page builder. You literally need zero knowledge in coding to build a landing page.

I have managed to hook you up with a **FREE** 14 Day trial of ClickFunnels, claim your free 14 Day trial here at http://clickfunnels.joshong.com.

BONUS: You will be getting an Affiliate Bootcamp Training as well for FREE (worth $997) if you sign up for the free trial.

What You Need to Do

If you have no idea where how to get started with affiliate marketing or an online business, our recommendation is you get started with this FREE Affiliate Bootcamp Training at http://affiliatebootcamp.joshong.com.

"Stopping advertising to save money is like stopping your watch to save time."

- Henry Ford

BONUS CHAPTERS

4 CORE FUNDAMENTALS OF SUCCESSFUL ONLINE BUSINESS

"If your business is not on the internet, then your business will be out of business."

- Bill Gates

There are numerous online business models you can adopt, but to be successful with an online business and get consistent and scalable results, you will need the following 4 fundamental elements:

1) Funnel

A funnel is a systemized process which will allow you to capture and turn your traffic into leads and eventually into buyers and loyal customers. A model which you can use is "AIDA" which stands for Attention, Interest, Desire, and Action.

Let us take Starbucks for an example, which could be applied to an online business as well.

Attention: Starbucks gains people's attention by constantly coming up with new drinks which is always placed on their home page of their website as well as occasional promotions.

Interest: Starbucks gets people interested by introducing new flavours.

Desire: With the new flavours, there is a desire in the customer as there is a sense of curiosity in the customer's mind, "how would that new drink taste".

Action: Starbucks then offers a reward program where the customers can collect points to redeem a free drink as well. Occasionally, Starbucks have one for one promotion which really is an irresistible offer. Knowing it's a buy one free one, often not the customer would bring another friend along as well to share that free drink with, in turn, Starbucks doubles their engagement, interest, and awareness.

CUSTOMER ACQUISITION FUNNEL

- ATTENTION
- INTEREST
- DESIRE
- ACTION

$

An example of an AIDA model which you could apply:

Attention: Grab people's attention by offering a free quiz to discover their purpose in life.

Interest: Get people interested with a sequence of strategic, insightful questions.

Desire: Let people know where they are at in life and how far are they in achieving their life purpose. Eventually comes their desire to achieve their life purpose (who doesn't want to achieve their life purpose, right?).

Action: Make an offer for an online course or live event where they would discover how to achieve their life purpose.

You can apply this framework based on the product or service you are offering.

"The aim of marketing is to know and understand the customer so well that the product or service fits him and sells itself."

- Peter Drucker

2) Filter

Different people have different needs, wants and spending power. You wouldn't want to be offering a make money online course to a person interested in weight lost. You would want to segregate your email list accordingly. By doing so, you would then exactly know which product to promote to which list of people.

Pro Tip: You would want to have a list to differentiate your potential customers as well people who have invested in your products before. This is because a person who has invested in one of your products before will have a much higher probability of purchasing from you again. That way it's easier to promote a much higher priced product to them.

3) Follow Up

The sale always comes after the follow-up. Do not expect people to purchase your product or service right away. Before a transaction can take place, your lead would need to know, like and trust you. This could be built through an email sequence by simply showing concern and adding value. Remember, the purpose of having an email sequence is to build a relationship and follow up with your lead. Once that has been done then only comes the sale.

You could have a telemarketing team to call and follow up with your leads as well. Of course, there will be a cost to hiring a telemarketing team. However, if the profit made is more than enough to cover the telemarketing cost, it will be worth your while.

4) Value Ladder and Product Mix

A value ladder is essential in any online or offline business. A value ladder basically is a tier of products or services which are of higher value and priced higher. In simple terms, a value ladder is where you further provide more value to your customer at the same time charge them a higher price. If you manage to deliver what you claim and your client is satisfied, I am very sure that they are more than willing to pay you more for delivering more value to them.

Sometime back I saw an advertisement on Facebook for a FREE 3-Hours Value Investing Masterclass where you would discover the secrets of how you can invest profitably using a proven system. So, after seeing this advertisement on Facebook, like any other person, I clicked on it and attended the 3-Hours free workshop. Yes, I did learn a lot and gained same value after attending the workshop. However, at the end of the workshop the speaker then pitched the upcoming 3-Days workshop called Value Investing Bootcamp for $3997. Me being as a potential customer, receiving tons of value after listening to the 3-Hours free workshop then felt very inclined towards signing up for the $3997 Value Investing Bootcamp. And eventually, I did end up paying $3997 to attend the Value Investing Bootcamp because I saw the value in it.

Take for example the value ladder of a company which teaches Value Investing in stocks:

Level 1: 3 Hours Value Investing Masterclass (FREE)
Level 2: Value Investing Bootcamp ($3997)
Level 3: Value Investing Mastery ($6997)
Level 4: Millionaire Inner Circle ($8897)

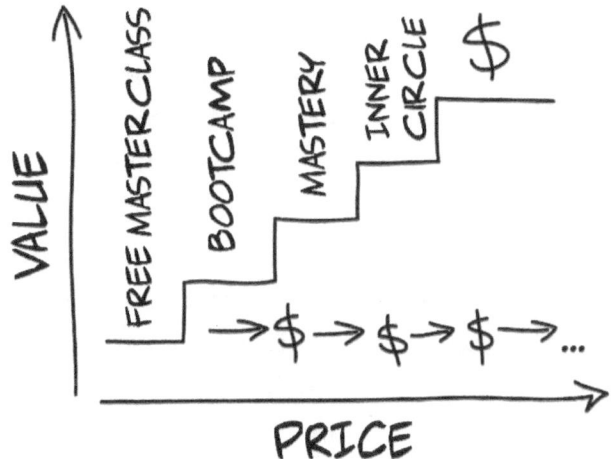

As you can see, by having a value ladder in place, you will then become more profitable. You do not only profit from a single sale but from the back-end as well.

Premium high-priced ticket items are a necessity for your online business success.

Think about it this way: If you set a goal to make $10,000 then you have two different ways to achieve that goal. You could sell 1000 products worth $10 each or sell 10 products worth $1000 each. The best strategy for many though is selling 10 items worth $1,000. It's not that convincing people to buy the larger item is easier, but it's the fact that you have to convince fewer people. This puts the odds in your favour. If you have an audience size in the thousands, then you're more likely to get at least ten sales.

Pro Tip: You are putting the same amount of effort and time for marketing a $10 and $1000 product, so why not promote a $1000 product?

Your product lot mix is also important because you can put various high-ticket items out there or a mixture of low and high-ticket items to reach your goal. You don't want to continue to promote the same product all the time. You need to promote different products that are within your niche. This way you'll have a higher chance of your audience wanting the products. So not only do you need different products, but you would want the products to be in the same niche.

TRAFFIC GENERATION

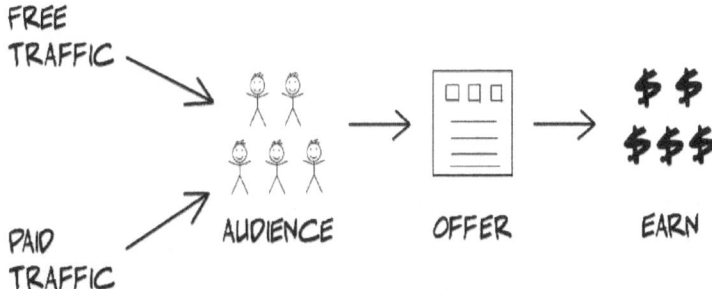

After your entire sales process is in place, from the landing page to the order fulfilment, your single most important area to focus on is generating traffic. You may have the best product in the world, but what is the use if nobody knows about your product. If nobody knows your product, how can they invest in it? Not only having people to see your product, you would need the "right" people targeted. If you try to sell everything to everyone, you will end up selling nothing to no one. You will need to identity the specific target market and you need to know your customers better than they know themselves. Essentially, there are two types of traffic, paid traffic and free traffic.

Paid Traffic Ideas
- ☐ Facebook Ads
- ☐ Instagram Ads
- ☐ Google Ads
- ☐ Bing Ads
- ☐ YouTube Ads
- ☐ Banner Ads
- ☐ Solo Ads: Udimi

Social media and search engine advertisements are the ones you commonly see when scrolling your news feed or searching something up on Google or YouTube. You can also purchase solo advertisements from Udimi in which the solo advertisers will send out an email with your offer to their email list.

Free Traffic Ideas
- ☐ Creating a YouTube video
- ☐ Posting on Facebook / Instagram
- ☐ Commenting in forums and discussion spaces like Quora and Reddit
- ☐ Blogging with SEO
- ☐ Guest Posting
- ☐ Press Release
- ☐ Local Directory (i.e Craigslist or Carousell)

Free Traffic vs Paid Traffic

If you actually realized, free traffic is not exactly "free". You will need to put in a lot of your time and effort into posting and writing reviews. The truth is, you will either be spending your time and effort or money in getting traffic. The downside of using a free traffic strategy is that your traffic not very consistent, hard to scale and certainly you will need to put in a lot of time and effort. The benefits of free traffic are that people will search you up automatically if you are well branded with good SEO, and you don't need to pay anything to obtain that lead.

Paid traffic, on the other hand, is a strategy once getting results, it becomes very predictable and scalable. Yes, you will require spending money on paid traffic, but your upside potential is immeasurably higher. The downside will be you losing money on paid traffic; however, just take it as a valuable lesson for you to tweak and launch your advertisement again. .

Pro Tip: Regardless if you are using free or paid traffic strategy, always remember to prioritise PROVIDING VALUE and not just only promoting your service or product.

What You Need to Do

1) Decide on which resource you would use for traffic generation:

- ☐ Time (Free Traffic)
- ☐ Money (Paid Traffic)

2) List down the platforms you would like to use for traffic generation:

"Whoever can spend the most to acquire a new customer, wins."

- Dan Kennedy

AFTERWORD

"Never give in. Never give in. Never, never, never, never—in nothing, great or small, large or petty—never give in, except to convictions of honour and good sense. Never yield to force. Never yield to the apparently overwhelming might of the enemy."

- Sir Winston Churchill

THOUGHTS

> *"Knowledge is only potential power. It becomes power only when, and if, it is organized into definite plans of action, and directed to a definite end."*
> **- Napoleon Hill**

I hope after reading this book you have found something useful, not just in starting an online business or earning passive income, but also helping you live your life by design. Imagine having more time to spend without your spouse, children, loved ones, friends, serving the community, hobbies and doing what you are truly passionate about.

If you are brand new and just starting out, I hope that you will take action and not give up. Earning your first dollar online is going to be the hardest thing for you, but once you make it, the second and your first thousand will be easier. I believe that most people never really achieve their dreams and aspirations; not due to the lack of resources, tools or talent, but because of the lack of commitment and desire.

Do you really desire to create a better future for you and your family? Take a step back and ask yourself this question, what will passive income and achieving financial freedom do for you? What lifestyle will it enable you and your family to have? Take some time to reflect on these questions and hopefully, that will strengthen your desire to achieve financial freedom.

Reading this book itself will not make you rich, that I can promise you. Only by taking action on the strategies shared in this book can you start to move closer towards your dreams. Majority of people who read books or attend seminars do nothing with the information and knowledge gained. Even after paying $1000 to $5000 for the seminar, they do not take any action and implement. If the sole intention of going to the seminar was to learn how to invest or make more money, why is their financial status still the same?

I truly believe that you are an action taker. You are not a mediocre person, but an extraordinary person who is seeking more in life. I believe in you, I believe you will generate passive income online and finally achieve financial freedom. Take massive action, keep on learning, never give up, never give in and keep on going.

Now you know the exact strategies for starting up five online businesses that generate passive income, go ahead choose one and get started right away! Don't let yourself get overwhelmed. Some of these ideas may seem easier to you than others, and that's perfectly okay. Some people will lean more towards the technicalities of affiliate marketing, or you may think that putting the money into designing an app is better suited to your talents. Just remember to settle down to put in the work, and you'll be making a passive income stream in no time! All it takes is a little research, a little inspiration, and some patience to stop the paycheck to paycheck cycle.

Stop procrastinating and TAKE ACTION! Knowledge is just potential power until you take action upon it!

Passive Income Tip: Identify the marketing strategy that works best for all of your businesses, then scale it!

May your entrepreneurship journey be a meaningful, fruitful and fulfilling one. Please leave a review for this book if it has added value to you, gave you new perspectives, helped you start an online business, earned passive income or helped you achieve financial freedom. I appreciate your time taken to read this book and I am enthusiastically waiting to hear your success story.

"The distance between your dreams and reality is called action."

- Unknown

"It's not about your resources, it's about your resourcefulness."

- Tony Robbins

RESOURCES

TOOLS AND RESOURCES

Screen Recorder
Movavi
Camtasia

Platform to Sell Course
Teachable
Udemy

Logo Creator
Fiverr
10alogo
LogoJoy

Platform to Sell Designer Items
CafePress
Zazzle
Merch by Amazon

Photo Editor

GIMP
Photoshop
PicMonkey

Stock Photos

Stocksnap.io
Upsplash
Pexels
Gratisography

Search Engine Optimization (SEO) Tools

SERanking

Wordstream Free Keyword Tool

SEO toolkit

Freelancers

Upwork
Freelancer

Web App Makers

Appery
AppMachine

Grammar Checker

Grammarly

Plagiarism Checker
PlagScan
CopyScape

Purchase Domain
GoDaddy
NameCheap

Website Hosting
HostGator
BlueHost

Affiliate Marketing
ClickBank
JVZoo
Amazon

Free Affiliate Bootcamp Training (Worth $997)
affiliatebootcamp.joshong.com

ClickFunnels: 14 Day Free Trial
clickfunnels.joshong.com

"If you don't design your own life plan, chances are you'll fall into someone else's plan. And guess what they have planned for you? Not much."

- Jim Rohn

ACKNOWLEDGMENTS

To my parents who shaped me into the person, I am today and supported me in all the decisions I have made in life. Thank you for being my pillar of strength.

To my brothers, Mozes and Samuel for bringing joy and laughter throughout the years.

To my buddy Anthony Tu, for guided me in writing my first book. You have always been there for me when I had any questions or concerns. Thank you for constantly supporting me in the making and publishing of this book.

Biggest thanks to Anna Long, Lean LaRowe, Rayson Choo, Ryan Teo, Khairul and Ksenia for proofreading and editing this book to its best version for you readers.

Last and not least, to all my dear readers who have taken your valuable time to read this book. It is such a great honor and privilege to be able to share my work with you. Thank you for giving me the opportunity to potentially change your financial status and the quality of your life forever. Thank you for your support of my work, and I believe that you are going to be living the life of your dreams while further adding value to others in your journey.

"Change is hardest at the beginning, messiest in the middle and best at the end."

- Robin Sharma

ABOUT THE AUTHOR

Joshua Ong is a coach, mentor, speaker, investor, serial entrepreneur and digital marketer. Over the last 5 years, he's been building multiple online and offline businesses that generate passive income.

It wasn't until he moved to Singapore alone to further his studies and having to bear the high cost of living, did he finally realize the importance of having multiple streams of income. With the power of the internet, he was able to leverage on it and harness the power to earn passive income online.

His life purpose is to develop individuals and businesses to unleash their full potential through digital marketing, entrepreneurship, and coaching. From going to seminars and meeting individuals such as Tony Robbins, Tom Ziglar, Robert Kiyosaki, Gary Vaynerchuk and Marshall Goldsmith, he believes in developing individuals to their fullest potential. Additionally, he strongly believes that we are put on this earth for a reason and we should be using our strengths and passion to fulfill our mission and purpose on this earth. He also believes in the importance of personal financial management and having more than one stream of income to achieve financial freedom.

Contact Joshua Ong at www.joshong.com or follow on Facebook (@joshuaongdream).

"You can have everything in life you want, if you will just help enough other people get what they want."

- Zig Ziglar

NOTES

NOTES

NOTES

NOTES

www.ingramcontent.com/pod-product-compliance
Lightning Source LLC
Chambersburg PA
CBHW031436210526
45464CB00005B/2228